The Visual Guide

Asperger's Syndrome in 12-16 Year Old Girls

by Alis Rowe

Also by Alis Rowe

The Girl with the Curly Hair - Asperger's and Me
978-0-9562693-2-4

The 1st Comic Book
978-0-9562693-1-7

The 2nd Comic Book
978-0-9562693-4-8

The 3rd Comic Book
978-0-9562693-3-1

The 4th Comic Book
978-15086839-7-1

The 5th Comic Book
978-15309879-3-1

Website:
www.thegirlwiththecurlyhair.co.uk

Social Media:
www.facebook.com/thegirlwiththecurlyhair
www.twitter.com/curlyhairedalis

The Visual Guide to

Asperger's Syndrome in 12-16 Year Old Girls

by Alis Rowe

Lonely Mind Books
London

For teenage girls on the autistic spectrum and their families and friends

hello

This age was probably the most terrifying and isolating time in my whole life. I felt so different from everyone and had no idea why (I wasn't diagnosed with Asperger's Syndrome (ASD) until I was grown up). I think it would've helped me a lot to learn that I had Asperger's Syndrome. Even if there weren't any solutions for coping with the trauma I was experiencing, I would've felt a million times more comforted knowing there was a reason for all the scary thoughts and feelings I was having and that there were others out there who thought and felt the same.

Although this book may not contain many strategies (my other books are a bit more strategy-based), it does I hope give plenty of insight into how a teenage autistic girl might be feeling. I hope a teenage autistic girl feels a lot less alone when she reads it and I hope the people around her develop more understanding and empathy for how she might be experiencing a very, very stressful time of life.

Alis aka The Girl With The Curly Hair

Contents

p11   **A late diagnosis**

p15   **Peers and friendships**

p31   **Introversion and extroversion**

p43   **Puberty and staying safe**

p53   **Masking**

A late diagnosis

It's common for females not to get their ASD diagnosis until adolescence (or often even later)

The Girl With The Curly Hair was always very "shy" and "sensitive" but didn't feel completely overwhelmed by these traits until she was a teenager

It's important to recognise that traits don't just suddenly develop, they're always there, but that they may not fully manifest until anxiety heightens (which is common during puberty and/or with the move to secondary school). Alternatively, traits may be masked by strategies that have been learned over time (consciously or subconsciously)

Why ASD traits may be more obvious after puberty

	Child	After puberty
Socialising	Young children are generally non-judgmental and accepting of everyone; social activities are usually very structured; parents have a lot of input into a child's friendships; interactions are simple and straightforward	A lot of peer pressure and competitiveness from teenagers ("fitting in" or being "the best" is important"); relationships are a child's own responsibility rather than their parents'; interactions are much more sophisticated and complex
Feeling 'different'	Young children usually can't recognise that they might be different	Someone might begin to recognise they are different as they go through puberty
Environment	Primary school is smaller and less busy	Secondary school is far larger, noisier, busier and more chaotic
Executive function	Children are strongly supported by their parents and teachers in being, for example, organised and flexible	More pressure on the child to be independent and to manage their own school diary, etc.

Peers and friendships

The Glass Jar Theory

After puberty, an autistic child might have intense feelings that they are 'different' and strongly recognise that they don't fit in

This is known as The Glass Jar Theory

The glass jar represents the social impairments that autistic people have

It's felt very strongly during puberty and beyond

The glass jar makes it very hard for the teenage autistic girl to connect with her peers

The autistic girl observes them all bonding with one another quite easily, whilst she is left out, or can't seem to connect in the same way

Neurotypical teenage girls tend to all want to be the same and to fit in

The Girl With The Curly Hair would try to fit in but it never seemed to work - she still felt very different and the other girls could tell that she was different

There may be lots of differences between teenage autistic girls like The Girl With The Curly Hair and teenage neurotypical girls... generally all to do with having completely different thought processes and experiences of daily life

The Girl With The Curly Hair is very sensitive to sensations. For example, she finds her friends' fragrances overpowering. Touch makes her very, very uncomfortable - it's an invasion of personal space and physically hurts. She can't bear for anyone to touch her

Another difference for The Girl With The Curly Hair is her strong need to be alone or to indulge in her solitary interests rather than socialising

Or her need for highly structured socialising where plans are kept to exactly

An autistic girl might have the same interests as her neurotypical friends but participates in them differently or experiences them more intensely...

This is what happened when The Girl With The Curly Hair's friends turned up at her house for the first time, without warning...

The Girl With The Curly Hair struggled to connect to her friends through her special interest, which was music and song lyrics. They didn't seem to be as interested as she was

Feelings of being different during teenage years can cause autistic girls to feel confused about their gender and sexuality

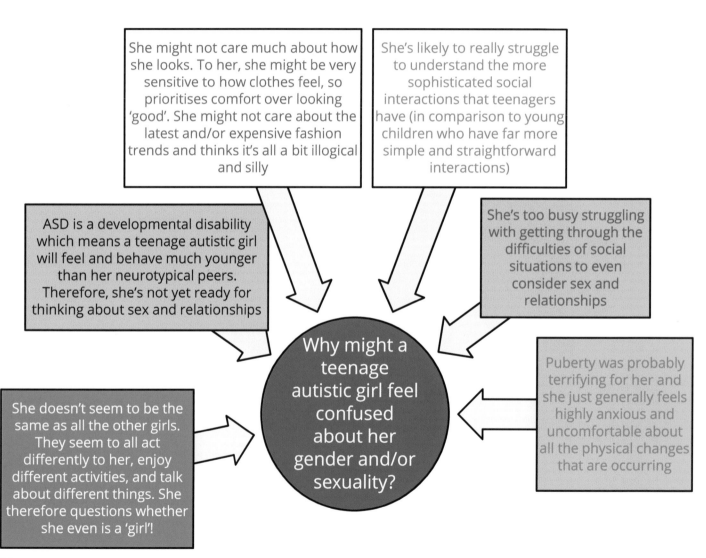

She might not care much about how she looks. To her, she might be very sensitive to how clothes feel, so prioritises comfort over looking 'good'. She might not care about the latest and/or expensive fashion trends and thinks it's all a bit illogical and silly

She's likely to really struggle to understand the more sophisticated social interactions that teenagers have (in comparison to young children who have far more simple and straightforward interactions)

ASD is a developmental disability which means a teenage autistic girl will feel and behave much younger than her neurotypical peers. Therefore, she's not yet ready for thinking about sex and relationships

She's too busy struggling with getting through the difficulties of social situations to even consider sex and relationships

Why might a teenage autistic girl feel confused about her gender and/or sexuality?

She doesn't seem to be the same as all the other girls. They seem to all act differently to her, enjoy different activities, and talk about different things. She therefore questions whether she even is a 'girl'!

Puberty was probably terrifying for her and she just generally feels highly anxious and uncomfortable about all the physical changes that are occurring

Unless peers are accepting and inclusive, a person like The Girl With The Curly Hair, who is different because she has ASD, is likely to experience the following:

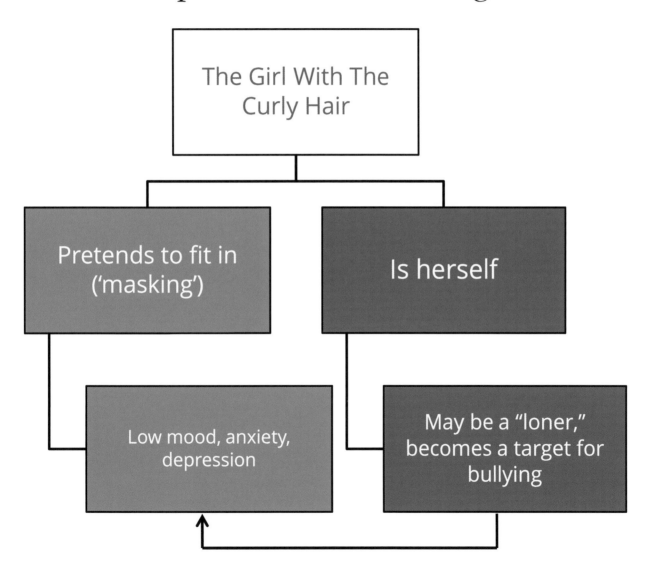

Therefore, to lessen the likelihood of poor mental health, it's very important that an autistic girl is able to:

• achieve a good balance between being herself and having to fit in (we all have to fit in at least a little bit, in order to work well as a society)
• spend time with people who accept her as she is (finding just one special person can be enough)

The Girl With The Curly Hair has some tips on finding the right sort of people to be around:

The teenage autistic girl might find it more successful to socialise with people in other age groups

- 'Differences' are normal for people of different ages / It's more expected that people will be different (so she will probably feel less different)
- It might help to socialise with people who are of the age that the teenage autistic girl emotionally and mentally feels

The teenage autistic girl might find it easier to socialise with people online

- However, she needs to be aware of internet safety and always discuss this with parents and carers
- She might find it useful to learn what is the 'correct' way to socialise online – for example, which websites are good for meeting people? What sort of things are acceptable to talk about? How will she know how to stay in touch with people?

The teenage autistic girl might find it easier to socialise with people who have similar interests

- She could find local clubs or websites based on her interests – there'll likely be a far greater diversity of people to befriend than the people in her class at school
- She can find people who like specifically the things that she likes about her interests, for example, analysing song lyrics, rather than just liking the interest generally
- Educating other people about what she knows (for example, coaching others, or setting up her own blog or video channel) can be a great way to feel connected to others
- Learning from other people (for example, by attending lessons, reading someone's blog, commenting on someone's video tutorial) can be a great way to feel connected to others

The teenage autistic girl will find it helpful to find empathetic and accepting people

- These people can be hard to find but they are out there! School can have limits on the sorts of people she meets

The teenage autistic girl could spend more of her spare time out in public

- Spending time in public such as at the library, the gym, coffee shops, etc. allows people to have the company of others without any pressure to be socialising, which can help the teenage autistic girl feel less isolated
- Friendships can develop naturally simply from seeing the same people regularly in the same settings

ASD support or social groups can sometimes be helpful for some autistic teenagers... but definitely not for everyone

Things about ASD support/social groups for teenage autistic girls and their parents to be cautious of	Positives of attending ASD support/social groups
• Parents might find these groups more helpful than their autistic children – so the main benefit of attending may be for the parents instead! • Lots of teenage autistic girls don't actually want to socialise, but their parents just think that they do, and think therefore that attending a group would be a good idea when it might not be • Some teenage autistic girls won't want their condition highlighted at all. It can take people some time to come to terms with it and it may not be a good idea to 'force' a teenager to learn about their ASD until she is ready • Socialising with other autistic teenagers can often just mean the social difficulties are doubled! • Parents and autistic teenagers sometimes just assume that it'll be easy for the autistic teenager to make friends with someone else just because they also have ASD. This is untrue	• The teenage autistic girl can learn more about herself • The teenage autistic girl can find others in similar circumstances who are likely to be having similar feelings • The teenage autistic girl might feel she can be open about how she is feeling, without being judged • These groups can help autistic teenagers to develop social skills

Introversion and extroversion

It might be very helpful to understand whether a teenage autistic girl is introverted or extroverted

In simple terms:

- Extroverts gain energy when they have social interactions
- Introverts lose energy when they have social interactions

There are lots of quizzes people can do to determine whether they're introverted or extroverted. This table might give you a rough idea which one you are:

	Introvert	Extrovert
Having conversations	Prefers to listen	Prefers to talk
Spending time with people	• Likes own company • If spending time with people, needs time to recharge afterwards	Enjoys being with other people
Persona	Quiet, thoughtful	A bit more bold and outgoing
Their own thoughts	Thinks before speaking	Likes to verbalise their thoughts

The Girl With The Curly Hair is very, very introverted. It made growing up and having friends even more difficult

Neurotypical teenage girls tend to be very extroverted - or, even if they're not - there's pressure to be so. Socialising is usually a big part of growing up for teenage girls

Neurotypical girl's interests*	The Girl With The Curly Hair's interests
• Boys • Shopping for clothes • Going to music concerts • Going on holidays • Doing hair and makeup • Doing team sports	• Playing computer games • Reading books • Writing stories and song lyrics • Walking the dog • Going on bike rides • Playing board games • Animals

*The Girl With The Curly Hair recognises that this is a stereotype. It's to be used for demonstrative purposes only. Always remember, everyone is different

A difficulty of having ASD is that the autistic girl, regardless of whether introverted or extroverted, will probably need a large amount of time alone or time to recharge

This time is very important for the autistic girl's wellbeing but can make building relationships very hard

Whilst other neurotypical teenage girls are spending time with each other outside of school and developing their friendship, the autistic girl is on her own... leading to her feeling isolated and left out, but desperately needing that time alone to recover from the stresses of daily life

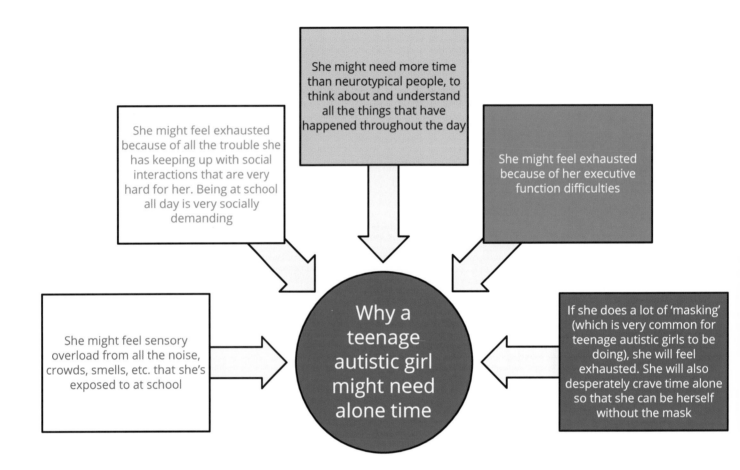

She might need more time than neurotypical people, to think about and understand all the things that have happened throughout the day

She might feel exhausted because of all the trouble she has keeping up with social interactions that are very hard for her. Being at school all day is very socially demanding

She might feel exhausted because of her executive function difficulties

She might feel sensory overload from all the noise, crowds, smells, etc. that she's exposed to at school

Why a teenage autistic girl might need alone time

If she does a lot of 'masking' (which is very common for teenage autistic girls to be doing), she will feel exhausted. She will also desperately crave time alone so that she can be herself without the mask

If the autistic girl is introverted, it helps to think about all the positive things that come from her being introverted, as opposed to everyone always highlighting the issue and 'forcing' her to be more talkative and sociable

It helps to work out if the autistic girl appears introverted because it's her personality or whether it's because she's genuinely struggling with social interactions because of her ASD

If it's her personality, usually it's best not to make her introversion a bigger deal than it is. If someone wants to encourage her to be more sociable, they ought to be sensitive, considerate and gentle rather than pushy, judgmental and forceful

The Girl With The Curly Hair's introversion was always brought up at home...

Dad was perhaps trying to be helpful in assisting her to maintain her friendships but it was coming over in the wrong way

Perhaps it would've been better if he had tried to understand her need for alone time and encouraged it, telling her how great she was at writing song lyrics! He could have helped her to understand how to communicate these needs to her friends so that they didn't assume she didn't like them (something he always worried about)

He could also have helped by trying to make social situations for her easier by, for example, making sure that she'd recharged enough before socialising, making sure that the socialising she did was structured, and agreeing on a 'getout' she could use with her friends should she suddenly want to go home

The Girl With The Curly Hair's introversion was always brought up at school...

Sadly, there's a lot of pressure on children (especially girls) to be sociable and chatty. Group work, class interaction, and after school clubs are all things that are encouraged

If someone isn't interested in these things, people can be quick to judge and assume there's something wrong

There's absolutely nothing wrong with being an introvert! Consider and talk about it as a positive trait rather than a negative one!

Having the fact that you are quiet highlighted over and over again, when that is just your natural personality, can really ruin your self-esteem

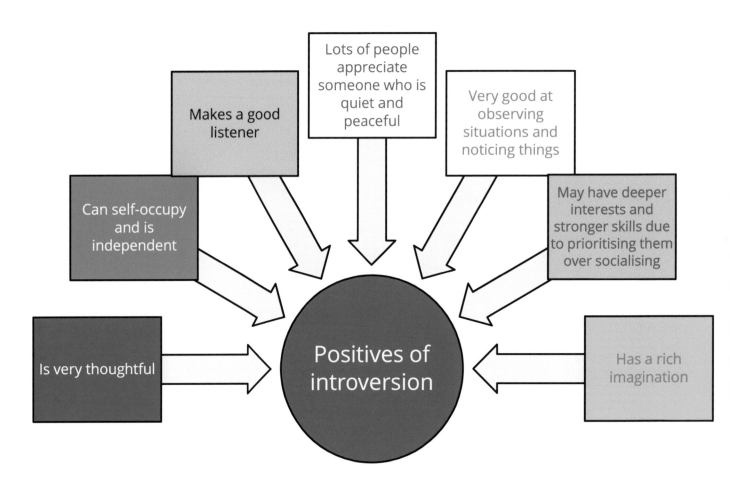

Puberty and staying safe

Puberty wreaks havoc with children's hormones

An autistic teenager will probably feel a lot more anxious and be prone to more frequent meltdowns during puberty

The Girl With The Curly Hair describes what puberty was like for her

Some autistic girls get on a lot better with boys

- Boys may be less judgmental
- Boys may be easier to read
- It might be more acceptable for boys to be 'loners', so an autistic girl might feel she can relate more closely to them
- Boys may prefer 'activities' to 'socialising' - so, for example, The Girl With The Curly Hair only liked her male friend because he played video games and went cycling with her

One problem is, a girl who gets on very well with boys, can cause conflict with other girls

Friendships with boys can be very innocent, but can easily be distorted or misunderstood by others and by the girl with ASD who can't see why it might be seen as a little unusual

It's very, very important that autistic girls realise that boys also go through changes during puberty

Some parents are really good at preparing their autistic daughters for adolescence but completely forget to talk to them about how their male friends and peers might also be changing

A male friend who is 'changing' can make the autistic girl feel lonely if she finds she can no longer relate to him because, for example, he begins to take a greater interest in socialising rather than the activities they used to do when they were younger (such as video games and bike rides)

The autistic girl needs to have a clear understanding of the sexual motives of boys who are also changing during puberty

Parents ought to maintain good communication with their teenage autistic daughters and always encourage them to talk about all things that are happening

Helping autistic girls to understand social situations is really, really important

Teenage autistic girls might find it easier to befriend people of a different age, which may make them vulnerable to older men taking sexual advantage

Autistic girls might also take their neurotypical peers at their word and then think that they too should be doing these things, without realising that people often say things that are untrue or that are exaggerated

Autistic girls may be more vulnerable to peer pressure, uncomfortable, and potentially highly dangerous situations - because they are trying to fit in, struggling to understand what people mean, and struggling to recognise boundaries

Other people may be more likely to take advantage of autistic people

Masking

Masking is what a lot of autistic girls do in order to:

- hide the difficulties they're having
- fit in with their neurotypical friends and peers
- avoid standing out
- stop family/friends from worrying about them
- pretend that they are OK because they think if they pretend enough that they will actually be OK

The problem is the strain of masking can eventually lead to mental health problems... and it can make relationships very, very difficult

It can also mean that other people (such as teachers, the GP, and even parents) can't see that anything is 'wrong' or don't believe that there are any 'problems'

The Girl With The Curly Hair is choosing her subjects for college. All her friends are excited about doing Biology... she isn't

The Girl With The Curly Hair is having her pulse taken

Mum and the Nurse wouldn't have known she was feeling so anxious if it wasn't for her elevated heart rate

The Girl With The Curly Hair hates lunchtime

The canteen is too noisy, too busy and smells too strongly

She feels completely overwhelmed but just goes along with what her friend wants

The Girl With The Curly Hair can't understand why her friends use the words that they do. It frustrates and confuses her. But she uses the same words them anyway

The Girl With The Curly Hair started puberty a long, long time ago. The whole experience terrified her, but her friends are having a completely different experience

It's really, really important to encourage teenage autistic girls to be themselves as much as possible and to teach them exactly how to be themselves whilst maintaining their friendships and avoiding hurting other people's feelings or getting bullied

There are some phrases you can use, which may not come intuitively, but they are very helpful

The Girl With The Curly Hair wished she'd known how to say these things when she was younger

Getting out of uncomfortable social situations (for example, when at school)

- "I've got to go to the shop before it closes"
- "I've got some homework to do"
- "I'm going to go and read my new book"
- "I just need some fresh air"
- "I need to nip to the toilet"

Declining invitations (if feeling too anxious to say "no" at the exact time, have a phrase you can use to give yourself extra time – no need to make immediate decisions)

- "I haven't got my diary on me right now. I'll check and get back to you"
- "I just need to check with my Mum. We might be doing something on that day"

Sensory (for example, with the nurse)

- "I'm really sensitive"
- "Please could you be extra gentle?"
- "I'm very anxious"
- "That's a bit too firm/bright/loud/[other] for me"
- "Please could you turn the music down?"

Different interests (for example, being invited somewhere you don't want to go; or a friend asking your opinion about something you don't like)

- "Thank you but it's not really my thing"
- "It looks/is great for you, but if it was me I'd prefer..."

Talking openly about the positive aspects of being different - and not always necessarily with regards to ASD - can help all people including neurotypicals, become more understanding, accepting and considerate

For example, there are advantages of being tall, short, overweight, underweight, speaking a different language, coming from another culture.. etc.

Reflecting on the positive aspects of ASD can help teenage autistic girls better appreciate their uniqueness

It may make them feel more confident about being themselves rather than feeling that they have to mask

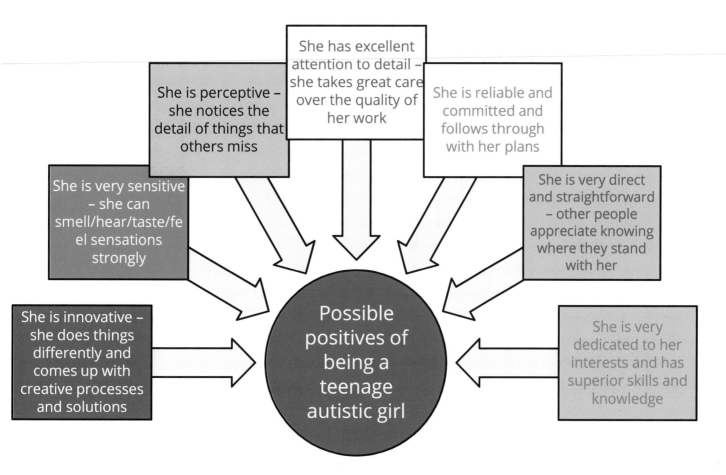

Summary

Puberty can be a very anxiety-provoking time that causes big changes in feelings and relationships

Autistic girls are likely to start feeling 'different' as they start puberty

Differences can be the way an autistic girl feels, how she sees a situation, the interests she has and how she participates in them, how she feels about clothes, scents, food... etc.

Finding the right sort of people to be around can really help an autistic girl feel less different and less lonely

Helping a teenage autistic girl find the right balance between being herself and fitting in is really important

Autistic girls are especially vulnerable and must learn to keep themselves safe and others must learn to help to keep them safe

Autistic girls are likely to have many positive traits

Autistic girls are likely to have particular gifts or interests ('special interests'), which should be encouraged, and can improve their self-esteem

There are lots of good things about being introverted, unless the teenage autistic girl isn't introverted and just appears so, because of her social difficulties (in which case she may need more support with her social skills). Work out just how sociable she'd actually like to be and support her in becoming that way

Many thanks for reading

Other books in The Visual Guides series at the time of writing:

Asperger's Syndrome
Asperger's Syndrome: Meltdowns and Shutdowns
Asperger's Syndrome Socialising & Social Energy
Asperger's Syndrome in 5-8 Year Olds
Asperger's Syndrome in 8-11 Year Olds
Asperger's Syndrome in 16-18 Year Olds
Asperger's Syndrome and Anxiety
Asperger's Syndrome: Helping Siblings
Asperger's Syndrome and Puberty
Asperger's Syndrome: Meltdowns and Shutdowns (2)
Adapting Health Therapies for People on the Autism Spectrum
Asperger's Syndrome and Emotions
Asperger's Syndrome and Communication
Asperger's Syndrome and Executive Function
Asperger's Syndrome: Understanding Each Other (For ASD/NT Couples)

New titles are continually being produced so keep an eye out!

Printed in Great Britain
by Amazon